YOUR COMPLETE PISCES 2023 PERSONAL HOROSCOPE

Monthly Astrological Prediction Forecast
Readings of Every Zodiac Astrology Sun Star
Signs- Love, Romance, Money, Finances, Career,
Health, Travel, Spirituality.

GW00458763

Iris Quin

Alpha Zuriel Publishing

Your Complete Pisces 2023 Personal Horoscope/ Iris Quinn. -- 1st ed.

*We are born at a specific time and place, and,
like vintage years of wine, we have the
characteristics of the year and season in which
we are born. Astrology claims nothing more.*
— CARL JUNG

CONTENTS

CHAPTER ONE

PISCES

Constellation: Pisces
Zodiac symbol: Fish
Date: February 19 – March 20
Zodiac element: Water
Zodiac quality: Mutable
Greatest Compatibility: Taurus and Virgo
Sign ruler: Jupiter and Neptune
Day: Thursday
Color: Lilac, Purple, Violet and Sea Green
Birthstone: Aquamarine

PISCES TRAITS

- Can be young and old at the same time.
- Considers everything to be a sign.
- Not sure it's a dream or reality
- Extremely romantic
- Prone to fantasizing.
- Has no limits.

PERSONALITY OF PISCES

It can be hard to describe a Pisces's personality because they tend to avoid standing out. Their conduct varies greatly depending on who they are around. Pisces are basically porous membranes that let things pass through them pensively. They are cognitive sea sponges. They are limitless. They tend to have a lot of different personalities, so it's difficult to figure out who they are.

Most Piscean characteristics (dreaminess, emotionality, imagination) are internal processes that are difficult to detect from the outside. This is because Pisces is an inward-looking sign. They are not self-absorbed, but they are self-absorbed.

A Pisces ultimately wishes to dissolve. To free themselves from their bodies and spread love to everything they touch. To live in the thin layer that's just above the material but not quite there. To live their lives as though they were love poems. To realize that reality and fantasy live next to each other on the same endless plane.

WEAKNESSES OF PISCES

The real weakness of Pisces is that they often cause their own trouble. They're a little obsessed with sorrow. Pisces want to feel everything deeply, and there is a tragic aspect to grief that Pisces truly enjoy. They would rather stew in a deep pit of despair than not feel anything at all. Pisces sometimes put themselves in self-defeating situations because they are looking for heart-wrenching emotional experiences. They then try to make it look like they were unwittingly hurt.

RELATIONSHIP COMPATIBILITY WITH PISCES

Based only on their Sun signs, this is how Pisces interacts with others. These are the compatibility interpretations for all 12 potential Pisces combinations. This is a limited and insufficient method of determining compatibility.

However, Sun-sign compatibility remains the foundation for overall harmony in a relationship.

The general rule is that yin and yang do not get along. Yin complements yin, and yang complements yang. While yin and yang partnerships can be successful, they require more effort. Earth and water zodiac signs are both Yin. Yang is represented by the fire and air zodiac signs.

Aries and Pisces

Pisces is too introverted and ethereal for Aries, who is a sign of activity and meets life without hesitation. Aries represents a risk that Pisces does not believe they are willing to assume. Pisces requires stability and peace in order to develop and flourish. These are traits

that Aries almost never possesses. To ensure the
success of this partnership, Aries must control their
impulses.

Taurus and Pisces

Although both Pisces and Taurus are yin, this
relationship is tough to establish. In order to
comprehend their various natures, they must invest a
great deal of effort. Taurus is basically a physical
being, and its life is centered around the physical. In
contrast, Pisces is a spiritual being. Although Pisces
requires the tangible, it is mostly concerned with
transcending it. If they can learn to complement one
another, they will both feel secure.

Gemini and Pisces

Pisces and Gemini are less likely to settle down
together than to break up. Gemini's volatility and
unpredictability will cause Pisces to feel
uncomfortable. Gemini cannot give Pisces the traits of
security and containment, even if it wanted to. Pisces
will complain about Gemini's inattention and
propensity to constantly escape the house. Regarding
fidelity, it is preferable to keep quiet.

Cancer and Pisces

Pisces and Cancer might develop a very strong emotional bond. Who will be responsible for their finances and practical matters? Both parties are willing to run the household, but neither will want to assume exclusive financial responsibility or obligations. The success of this connection will rely on how this ground is managed.

Leo and Pisces

Pisces and Leo are capable of forming an exceptional partnership that should not be taken for granted. This is a yin-yang relationship, and they will need to address the seeming contradictions (such as that Leo focuses on the self while Pisces focuses on others). However, they have everything necessary to meet both of their requirements. Leo possesses enormous strength and will provide Pisces with the necessary security and safety. Pisces will shower Leo with accolades, praise, tenderness, and thanks.

Virgo and Pisces

For a partnership between Pisces and Virgo to be successful, Virgo must learn to control its critique

nature. Pisces is so sensitive that it cannot tolerate
being criticized for errors. In this instance, Pisces will
retreat into their fantasy world, and Virgo will be
excluded from the connection. This is an unhealthy
situation, and it may be simpler for them to split. If both
parties choose to continue the relationship, these
concerns can be resolved. Virgo and Pisces are at
opposite extremes of the health axis, yet they might
find common ground in their desire to do good.

Libra and Pisces

A relationship between Pisces and Libra will be
challenging to achieve. Pisces is too emotional and
sensitive for Libra's analytical abilities. The alluring
nature of Libra is insufficient to satisfy Pisces' yearning
for emotional security. In addition, Libra's persistent
uncertainty will increase Pisces's sense of insecurity.

Scorpio and Pisces

Both Pisces and Scorpio feel emotionally confined
and understood in a relationship between them. Both
Pisces and Scorpio place a high value on the emotional
and spiritual sides of life, which they fully
comprehend. Scorpio's explosive urges are subdued by
Pisces' gentleness.

Sagittarius and Pisces

Pisces and Sagittarius can build a committed and enjoyable partnership that is mutually beneficial. Pisces will need to learn not to require Sagittarius to always exhibit their devotion excessively. So that Pisces doesn't feel concerned, Sagittarius will have to learn to prioritize Pisces' demands. As for the rest, this connection has a positive outlook.

Capricorn and Pisces

Capricorn will provide Pisces with an incredible world because, from the outset, Capricorn will solve all problems, anticipate potential disputes, and maintain the home. Pisces will believe it has discovered the love of its life and will lavish Capricorn with extravagant gifts and passionate kisses. However, Pisces must learn to endure Capricorn's frequent emotional iciness.

Aquarius and Pisces

Pisces and Aquarius can create a committed and pleasurable relationship if they respect one another's differences from the start. Tolerance is necessary. Pisces needs to understand that Aquarius needs to be

alone, and Aquarius needs to try to show more
emotion.

Pisces and Pisces

In a relationship, two Pisces will have a mystical
knowledge of each other's emotions. Affectionate
displays will be commonplace between the two.
However, disputes can emerge when each party
expects the other to provide protection. One of them
must be accountable for their financial responsibilities
and material security.

LOVE AND PASSION

Every time a Pisces starts a new relationship, they
forget about the ones that didn't work out and give it
their all. For them, getting to know their partner on a
profound level is a gradual but intriguing process that
culminates in total togetherness. They enjoy
surrounding themselves with an aura of sensuality and
istication, and they never stop to impress their
it other with thoughtful gifts and delectable

Those in a relationship with a Pisces become a part
of the Pisces' inner circle. They feel extremely special
and are showered with attention.

Pisces creates an emotional bond by fusing their
bodies with those of their loved ones. They view sexual
activity as a sublime experience. Their love is as gentle
and consistent as a gentle drizzle. Physical contact
allows for a deepening of their relationship.

They quickly develop dependence on their partner,
which can occasionally result in a mismatch. They
want the other person to be fully devoted and for both
of them to gain emotionally from the exchange. A
secure partnership provides them with confidence and
contentment.

MARRIAGE

All Pisces desire to share their lives with their ideal
partner. Some of them keep their honeymoon going for
as long as they can after they get married. Their love
and commitment make their marriage a magical
experience.

For others, though, marriage is a huge letdown because it doesn't turn out the way they thought it would. Because they can't solve the problems that every couple has, they give up at the first sign of trouble. This puts their relationship in danger. Pisces would be better off if they gave up their dreams and started living in the real world.

Women usually put the needs of their partners ahead of their own. They are loving mothers who put their families before themselves.

Men, on the other hand, are sentimental, yet they are always willing to lend a helping hand and have plenty to offer their spouse and children.

CHAPTER TWO

PISCES 2023 HOROSCOPE

Overview Pisces 2023

Jupiter begins the year in the 2nd house of Aries for Pisces inhabitants, then moves to the 3rd house of Taurus in May. This brings you wonderful financial resources and family well-being for the year's first three months. The star in May would then impact your short-term travel plans and your relationship with your siblings. Saturn, the renowned disciplinarian, will transit your 12th house for the first quarter of this year before moving to your Ascendant house.

Your overseas travels and spiritual pursuits will likely be significantly hampered. As you return to your home base, the emphasis will be on your overall well-being and health, and Pisceans will likely experience health issues for the next three months.

Regarding the outer planets, Uranus will transit Taurus' 3rd house in 2023, while Neptune will transit your Ascendant all year. Pluto begins the year in your 11th house of Capricorn and then moves to your 12th house of Aquarius later in May-June.

With such a flurry of activity in the zodiac sky, your life is bound to be exciting in the coming year.

Venus, the planet of love, will ensure that your love and marriage paths are unobstructed in the coming year. Even long-distance partnerships would benefit you these days. There would be no flirting or infidelity on the part of the Pisceans, and you would be continuously linked up with a companion. After several difficult times, you will reclaim your partner's love and confidence. Mars also ensures that your love life or marriage is peaceful and without incident.

Pisces folks are expected to do well in their careers in the coming year. Because Jupiter is Aspecting your 7th house, you will be more compatible at work. This year will bring you success in all of your professional endeavors. Your income flow would improve, and you would have more financial options owing to your side hustles.

2023 is not going to be a fantastic year for Piscean people's health. Simply because the planets are not

very well aligned and Jupiter would occasionally bring
health problems for Pisces, especially in the second
half of the year. Saturn in your Ascendant house
beyond the first quarter of the year might exacerbate
your health issues. Pisceans are more likely to get
regular headaches or migraines, and some of you may
contract infectious infections throughout the year.
Take precautions and care for your overall health and
well-being.

Pisceans' financial situation will improve a bit this
year. You would succeed in business and services,
bringing in a steady income stream. Despite the inflow,
savings would be a significant hurdle, with undesired
expenditure coming in from all directions. Rahu, which
is the Moon's node in your financial house, will cause
you to have a lot of money problems this year.

Your fourth house of Gemini has no major
planetary transits this year; thus, family life will be
mediocre. Saturn and Jupiter would ensure peace and
harmony in your world. Your ideas about family and
its evolution are currently taking shape. Your family
grows as new members join you through marriage or
birth. Throughout the year, you should maintain a
balance between your personal and professional
standing. Saturn brings stability and maturity to your
family life and takes care of the fundamental

necessities. And Jupiter will bestow upon you ease and all the conveniences of life.

Pisces people have a lot of long-distance travel planned for them this year. Foreign travel would benefit you by expanding your knowledge and making money. Jupiter promotes some travel beyond the first quarter of the year for enjoyment, adventure, and pleasure. However, Pisceans are advised to use caution when travelling during the period, as health concerns and accidents may emerge. Also, exercise caution while making financial arrangements for your travel plans.

The beginning of the year would be ideal for performing religious acts. You'd be expanding your spiritual knowledge this year with Jupiter in your 9th house. For the time being, you will be more spiritually inclined and dedicated to spiritual work. Participate in social and charitable activities to strengthen your confidence in people. Around the end of the year, certain Pisceans may travel on pilgrimages to seek the blessings of sages or saints.

The coming year may appear tough and tight, but if you just go with the flow, life will be easier and happier. You will be blessed pleasantly. Appreciate the good things, be thankful, and share them with others in need. Do whatever provides you with peace and

harmony in various facets of your life. Spread joy,
perform one good deed per day, and be safe.

January 2023

Horoscope

You evolve in a relationship setting that makes you feel safe and secure. Capricorn's energies help you avoid nasty surprises and bring you the right people. When problems come out of the blue, they bring you the solution. With the weather being so nice, you have every chance of getting what you want. But in the long run, all this work may seem like a waste of time. You feel like you're spinning your wheels.

Mars forces you to leave your comfort zone when it is in Gemini. You seem adorable in his eyes. He makes you promises, but you can't be sure he'll keep them. Ask for advice from someone you can trust and who is competent before making a decision that could later be embarrassing.

Love

Your love is on hold. You have a hard time putting your feelings into words, which makes it seem like you don't care about your loved ones. This month, you'll know where you are thanks to Venus passing through your zodiac sign on the 28th. It appears that your love life is off to a good start and heading in the right direction.

There isn't much excitement going on this month. You're being compelled to take stock of your sentiments and your identity. What you want and don't want is crystal clear by the end of the month.

Single Pisces, You'll feel like time is going by slowly because your love won't be as bright until the 28th. From this date on, the impossible can happen. Someone you know finally tells you what they care about and want to do.

Career

Everything is going according to plan. The only thing left to do is to do what you're already good at: daily maintenance. In spite of this, don't rest on your laurels. Keep your guard up, and don't put your faith in anyone who promises you anything. This month, Pisces, dare to say no with all your might! You won't become a brutal person, but you will have a keen sense of judgement.

During the month, job prospects are not very good. You would have to work very hard for not much in return. Gains that were expected wouldn't happen, but the work environment might stay good and stress-free.

Also, travelling wouldn't bring you the benefits you'd hope for, though a trip to the South might give you some benefits. Having contacts wouldn't help, so it would be best to rely mostly on your skills to deal with challenging situations. And, given how things are going this month, this skill will help you in the end.

Finance

On the astrological front, Jupiter guards this industry. Even though you don't always get money, your financial situation is improving.

Your financial situation is looking up this month. There is a good probability that an elderly friend could provide a significant benefit to you. A business alliance or professional affiliation with a woman will likely bring you even more success. This has the potential to bring in a lot of money.

It would be an excellent time to start new businesses and invest. It's time for those with such intentions to put them into action. Also, there would be a good chance that banks and other financial institutions would approve any loan requests already in the works or any new proposals for new loans.

Health

This is an excellent month for your health. The stars are aligned in your favor, so you don't have much to worry about. Even people prone to long-term conditions like rheumatism and digestive tract problems will feel better.

When your body absorbs all the nutrients from the food you eat, you will feel good about your health and look good. The powers of reproduction will also be at their best, making life a good time. Not only will you be very active and full of energy, but your mind will also be in good shape. A nice month that would require you to do very little work.

Travel

The stars don't look good for travel this month, so you shouldn't expect to get what you want. People whose jobs or businesses require travel a lot may find themselves in an unenviable situation that doesn't live up to their hopes.

People in sales and marketing would do much worse, and even facing South, which is usually the best direction, wouldn't help. Also, there is a good chance that business trips outside the country will not live up to expectations.

Insight from the stars

Keep your promises and kind words to yourself this month. Don't be fooled by outward appearances. This will keep you from making unrealistic plans that jeopardize your long-term success. Your financial situation will be better this year than the previous year.

February 2023

Horoscope

Pisces, Capricorn, and Taurus sign energies promise you their goodwill protection. In order to help you progress, these pragmatic energies create favorable conditions. This month, you're living in an astrological environment that supports the completion of your goals. The appropriate individuals are drawn to you at the right time because of your personality. In an ideal world, everything works out perfectly.

The New Moon in your zodiac sign on the 20th will reawaken your senses. It gives you brilliant ideas. You'll still have to deal with Mars' dissonances in Gemini, though, because they're taking on a life of their own this month. To keep what you've worked for, you need to be innovative and refuse to give in to temptation.

Love

When Venus is in your sign, your world gets back
on track. Resumption of pleasant and productive
discussions. Love is restored to your relationship with
understanding and generosity. Watch out for promises
that come from outside of your comfort zone, though.
Nothing about them implies that they'll be trusted or
appreciated.

When you're in a relationship, it's hard to know
what to expect. The mood is tense and distant at times.
Once again, Earthly energies force you to take stock to
understand where you are in relation to the larger
picture.

Single Pisces, you attract attention with your
seductive powers. Your charisma sways hearts. If you
want a happy, healthy relationship, give more weight
to the person who cares about you and ignore the
person who makes promises.

Career

People who know your abilities and have complete
faith in you are looking out for this area and its growth.
Life has suddenly become a lot easier. You take your
work seriously and rely on your gut instincts to make
decisions. Unfortunately, the pleasant weather here
won't protect you from the tiny inconveniences the
outside world offers. When a problem emerges, Pisces,

don't worry about it. Everything will be OK if you just
speak what's on your mind.

According to the horoscope, your professional
prospects look bleak this month. You'd have to put in a
lot more effort for a lot less money if you increased
your workload. The situation would be somewhat
made up for by a pleasant and stress-free place to work.
But not any more than that.

You wouldn't get the benefits you were hoping for
from travel, but a trip to the West would bring you
some benefits. Not enough to make up for everything,
it needs to be said. The people you know won't be much
help, making a difficult situation even harder. Also,
don't do anything illegal because that could worsen
your problems.

Finance

On the money side, if you come across a dead end,
don't worry. It won't last long. Based on their
predictions, the stars don't look good for your money
this month. You might have a mean streak and be
persuaded to take advantage of your employees,
subordinates, or just people lower on the social ladder
for your own gain. Your efforts to do these things
would be met with strong opposition, which could put
you in a terrible situation.

So, use a firm hand to stop these behaviors. Also, people who work in international trade could have a rough time. In fact, most of you would have to work very hard to reach your goals, and even then, you might not get very far. A bad spell for you, during which it wouldn't be a good time to invest or start something new.

Health

This month, the stars are in your favor regarding your health, so you have nothing to worry about. Your body would get the most out of the food you eat, which could show in your glowing health. Your ability to reproduce would also be at its best.

Not only will you be very busy all month, but you'll also be in such good shape that your life will be much richer and fuller in every way. There is a chance that you will work too hard. But you can get around this by making a smart plan that doesn't put too much stress on you. Overall, it's a good month that lets you enjoy life.

Travel

The stars don't look good for you on this score this month, so there is a huge possibility of disappointment coming from your travels. People who work in marketing or sales and travel a lot as part of their job or business would have a hard time. Even trips in the best direction, which is West, might not be enough to fix the situation.

A trip abroad would not be a good idea the way things are going. In fact, a trip like this could sometimes make your losses much worse. Also, travelling this month wouldn't be near as fun as it usually is. You also wouldn't get any new opportunities from travelling.

Insight from the stars

Decision-making could be on the cards for you this month. Don't be swayed by the beautiful promises of others. Pay attention to your gut instincts because they are your most reliable compass. A strong sense of romance permeates the air. Spending time with your lover will be enjoyable for both of you. Knowing that you have a lot of love in your life is the best feeling in the world.

March 2023

Horoscope

Saturn is moving into your zodiac sign this month, which is a significant event. This is it if you're looking for an austere but motivating energy. Capricorn and Taurus energies are associated with this; therefore, you'll gain knowledge, experience, and abilities as a result of it. The depth of your relationships with others will increase. Over time, they will become noticeable.

Saturn will also assist you in your endeavor by ensuring you only keep people who will contribute to your growth. This month, Mercury will be in your sign, and he will advise you to take a step back and evaluate the situation before making a decision. When the Full Moon in Virgo appears on the 7th, it's an excellent time to sit back and watch before taking action.

Love

Planets in friendly signs help you take care of this area in a practical way. You adjust to new situations and people while subtly moving away from what doesn't work for you. From the 17th, Venus brings you together with people who care about the same things you do.

Mars in Gemini is a source of discord, and the Full Moon on the 7th makes it even worse. Your relationship goes through a rough patch that can last for a long time. Encourage your partner to take a break from the things that annoy them to avoid these problems.

Single Pisces, Mars is in Gemini, which makes it hard for you to get along with the people you love. Encounters fade away into the universe. On the 17th, the weather improves, and on the 26th, Mars in Cancer confirms this.

Career

When Saturn moves into your sign, it shows how experienced you are and makes you more mature. The star of wisdom makes you stop and think about what is really important. Your goals change over time. They get right to the point. But this transfer can change the way you feel. So, don't worry too much if you feel a little down this month. Don't push yourself more than you need to because it won't help your career.

The way the stars are aligned in front of you doesn't look good for your career. There would be a lot of short trips that wouldn't bring the expected benefits. On the other hand, a trip to the North would be helpful. During this time, it's not likely that people you know will be able to help you much.

So, it would be a good idea to trust in your ability to solve problems. But there are reasons to think that the working conditions and atmosphere would stay pretty good. This would be a big reason to be happy. Overall, it is a month when you must be careful with several sensitive matters.

Finance

When it comes to money, this area is still driven by Jupiter. Money doesn't always come in. In this situation, you must be very careful with your budget, especially around the 7th.

Even though you'll be hanging out with many bright and spiritually gifted people this month, it won't be good for your finances. There is a good chance that most of you will have to work hard to achieve your goals, and even then, you might not get very far.

The climate would also not be suitable for making investments or starting new businesses. They might get stuck. Also, banks or other financial institutions would unlikely approve any pending loan applications or requests for further advances. Also, people who do business overseas would probably have to deal with adversity.

Health

This month, the stars don't look too good for your health, so you'll have to pay much more attention to your well-being. Even if you eat a healthy diet, it's possible that your body won't be able to do much with it.

In other words, your daily meals would be devoid of nourishment, and you'd show signs of malnutrition similar to starvation. This should not be a reason for concern but rather a wake-up call to focus on corrective actions. These could have a significant impact on your health if properly implemented. You can get through this hard time if you take care of yourself.

Travel

Since the stars are in a good mood to bless you this month, you'll reap many benefits from traveling. Traveling for business or pleasure is an option open to everyone, not just those who are accustomed to frequent travel as part of their job duties. You may also be presented with new possibilities as a result of this.

There are strong indications that most of the travel will be by train or road, with a small amount of air travel. The North would be the best direction to travel in. Those that travel overseas are nearly assured of having a wonderful experience. In fact, this is an excellent time to do so.

Insight from the stars

As time passes, planets in friendly signs help you feel like you belong in your universe again. What's going on with your friends? It's perfectly natural. Keep your distance, and don't try to make up ground. Some of your friends will betray you, so you should be careful about who you let into your circle of friends.

April 2023

Horoscope

As a result of the influences originating from Pisces and Taurus, you feel like you are being thrust into the real world. As they continue to sort out your relationships, they strengthen the ones that had been loose. You'll be surrounded by comforting and soothing energy when you're with folks you can trust. They are the ideal people to help you achieve your goals. You make the appropriate decisions based on their advice and rationale.

As a result, Mars in Cancer helps you to focus on what you enjoy and what is best for your life. Venus in Gemini between the 12th and the 30th is the only issue. This negative impact can be lessened if you accept the idea that you have the choice to decline anything that does not suit your preferences.

Love

Your relationships grow in a calm and stable environment due to the good vibes of Venus and Mars. You find peace that brings out the best in you. Things get worse after the 12th. Use your courage to say no to things that bother you.

Everything about your relationship is fine until the 11th. Then things get tricky! This month, Mercury supports in-depth discussions. It aids you in dealing with a difficult situation and finding a lasting solution.

Single Pisces, planets in friendly signs put you in touch with people who are attracted to your charm. Even a bad genius could try their luck, though. If you talk about important things, they'll reveal their true motives and make the right choice.

Career

As time passes, this area gets to a speed where it can keep going. There is success. You work very hard at what you do. Everything is fine, but you don't seem very motivated. Have you taken a look at what you do? Perhaps. In the meantime, there would be a lot of hard work, but the benefits wouldn't match the work. Also, travel is mentioned, but again, this wouldn't live up to expectations in a meaningful way.

Contacts won't help you much either during this time, though some female coworkers or friends will try to promote your professional achievements. It would be better to rely mostly on your skills and hard work. A month where you'd have to work hard to keep going.

Finance

On the money side of things, things are getting better. There is money coming in. You get many rewards for all your work. Before you spend money without thinking, look at how much you have and the level of comfort it provides.

But even if you worked very hard, the way things are now, you wouldn't get the results you expected or planned for. There are also no promising signs of starting an expansion or a new business.

If you want a loan from a bank or other financial institution, your project is likely to move slowly and get in the way. There is also a risk that people doing business with people outside your country or with a different legal status will encounter difficulties and even lose money.

Health

It will be a good month in which you will be healthy and thrive from the food you eat. This means that you are in good health and your body can use the food you

eat. Any sudden, severe illness should be treated right
away.

If you treat these symptoms as soon as you notice
them, you can be sure that nothing terrible will happen.
If you were to test your reproductive ability, you would
be pleased to find that it is way above average. A good
month that doesn't need much of your attention.

Travel

Since the stars aren't aligned in a good way, this is
not a good month for making money from travel. You
could get hurt or have some other physical trouble
during your travels. Because of this, you should be
careful.

Also, your job or business would require you to
travel for a certain amount of time this month. This
would not work out very well, though. Even trips to the
best direction, the West, would not help. Some of you
might go on a trip outside the country, which wouldn't
help you achieve your goals.

Insight from the stars

Stability is gained when you surround yourself with
people who are serious about their work. Frivolous
people cause you to fall down a steep hill. You won't

get lost if your conversations have substance. You will meet new people and have a beneficial impact on everyone's life.

May 2023

Horoscope

Reconnecting with your loved ones is made possible by Taurus and Cancer's soothing and supportive energies. Some of the people who have been away may return to you. Your relationships are trustworthy because you chose them yourself.

When Jupiter moves into Taurus on the 17th, the ideas driving your conversations for the past few weeks will be more stable. He hopes that you will spend more time studying them. He encourages you to accept them if you're on board. With the help of the lucky star and evolution, you can improve your life by adding more comfort and safety. Venus and the Sun in Gemini cast the only shadows on the board, but only briefly. The only way to permanently eliminate it is to be adamant about it.

Love

Venus in Gemini stirs up trouble until the 7th. The energies of Taurus and Cancer make it easy for you to choose peace and safety. The Sun in Gemini will start to question this choice on the 22nd unless you stop listening to the siren song.

Your relationship finds its way and becomes more real. You manage to get your point across and take charge of the situation again. But until the 7th and after the 22nd, you'll have to be disciplined with yourself if you don't want things to get out of hand.

Single Pisces, You are surrounded by people who want to help you, but a lousy person keeps trying to throw you off. Don't move away from your positions if you want to get rid of them.

Career

If your motivation has been low, a smile should help. This month's discussions are centered on your personal and professional growth.

Some people extol the virtues of your abilities. The others want to know what you can do. If you think things aren't going well, you should wait. As time passes, your partners will be clearer about what they want. If someone makes you an exciting offer, don't look any further, Pisces. Think about it carefully and choose wisely.

There would be a lot of travel, but it wouldn't go as
planned, though a trip to the South might be helpful.
People you know wouldn't be as beneficial as usual
either. Because of this, you should rely mostly on your
skills and resources. Persistent caution in dealing with
difficult situations is called for throughout this month.

Finance

When it comes to money, this sector is doing
exceptionally well, which shows how hard you have
worked to get there.

Since the stars are in your favor, you should do very
well financially this month. People who do business
with other countries or across state lines would do very
well and gain a lot. Most of you would be able to get
the planned gains from your current operations during
this time.

Also, this would be a good situation for people who
want to grow their businesses or start new ones. Those
with loan requests pending with any bank or financial
institution will obtain the required loans. It's important
to remember that working with women in business or
the workplace would be beneficial.

Health

A month in which you're almost sure to be in good
health. People prone to long-term problems like
rheumatism and too much gas in the digestive tract will
feel much better. They only need to use the usual
amount of care to get relief from their illnesses.

The food you eat will feed your body and keep you
in great shape. You will have above-average
reproductive vitality, giving you a healthy mind and
body. There are a few reasons to take a sore throat
seriously if you have one. The rest should go well.

Travel

The signs from the stars make it clear that there isn't
much chance of making money. People whose jobs or
businesses take them around a lot will not get much out
of the exercise. Even for the rest of you, your business
trips wouldn't bring in much money. Even going in the
best direction, which is South, would not change the
situation.

You could worsen your problems by going on
expensive trips abroad that would not help you achieve
your goals. This could make things even worse for you.
Under these circumstances, you should keep your plans
as simple as possible.

Insight from the stars

The quality of your life is steadily improving, but nasty people refuse to change. You can keep them out of your sphere of influence by acting cold and distant. Everything in your life has a purpose, and you must accept this. Instead of doubting everything, have faith in the process.

June 2023

Horoscope

The lucky placement of Jupiter in Taurus makes it easier for you to achieve your goals, which were previously limited by strict rules. This comfort is shown by living a less austere way of life. The presence of Uranus in your chart means that blessings from the sky will also help your daily life.

This month, you'll get great rewards for all your hard work. Slowly but surely, you find the balance you need. Also, how people act and feel toward you might be a pleasant surprise. Still, the dissonances that come from Gemini can ruin this friendly atmosphere. You can argue to make them happy, but it will work better to stay in your world and wait for it to pass.

Love

During this month, Venus has little effect on your life. She, on the other hand, has an effect on others. All of a sudden, the roles have been switched. Others will

use their inventiveness to their advantage to entice or
satisfy you. So you don't have to do anything but
accept the gifts and words of love that are meant for
you.

Even though things are looking better by the day,
an overflow is still possible. If you want harmony in
your life this month, don't budge from your principles.
Everything returns to normal at the end of the month.

Single Pisces, Your admirers use various creative
methods to entice you. If you had doubts about your
ability to seduce, they would be gone this month. You
decide what to do next!

Career

Your work life gets easier and more comfortable,
and you may get more responsibilities. At the time, you
can tell you won't be able to do it or that the weight is
too much for your small shoulders. Pisces now is not
the time to talk badly about your skills and strengths.
Instead, tell yourself repeatedly that you are where you
should be and that everything is fine.

Even if you worked really hard, you're unlikely to
get anywhere near the goals you set out to achieve. The
way things are going, this just isn't going to happen.

Travel also wouldn't give you what you were
hoping for, but a trip to the West might bring you some

luck. There are also reasons to think having contacts won't help you much. So, it would be best to rely on your skills and hard work. Not a good time and you should only get through it if you know how to handle difficult situations well.

Finance

On the money side, don't let this part of your life run you. Instead of giving this job to someone else, keep a close eye on it.

The signs from the stars don't give you much reason to be optimistic about your money this month. You might find that you're working hard to achieve your goals, but you're not getting anywhere because of the bad things that keep happening. On top of that, the environment would not be favorable for expanding operations or starting new businesses.

People who work in the arts, like painters, writers, sculptors, and so on, should be prepared for a particularly tough time. It's preferable to keep a low profile for the time being until the bad times are past.

Health

The way the stars are aligned this month is a clear blessing for your health. In this case, you have nothing to worry about. In fact, your body will get the most out of the food you eat, putting you in the best shape possible. This would mean having a healthy body and mind. You'd be able to maintain a high level of physical and mental activity.

And those who like to judge how well they reproduce will be pleased to find that they are much better than average. Any kind of infection in the chest or lungs must be treated immediately. If this is done, there is no danger or reason to worry. If you didn't do this, your problems would get much worse. Those are little things that you should not ignore.

Travel

This month, you should try to travel as little as possible since doing so won't get you what you want and may even worsen things. There are signs that people whose jobs or businesses require them to travel a lot will be disappointed.

Even trips to the best direction, the West, wouldn't help. People who trade with other countries or have any kind of business with other countries may find, much to their dismay, that their trips abroad turn out to be useless.

Insight from the stars

Putting on an air of being distant keeps intruders
away and encourages others to show how honest they
are. Keep going in this direction. It will help you find
the balance you want. You will finally be happy with
the results of your investments last year.

July 2023

Horoscope

Your group is like a close guard who cheers you on
when you need it. They help you make good decisions
by giving you good advice. So, you walk in a planned
and organized way toward a comfortable success. Your
plans for reaching your goals are clear. Jupiter gives
you the opportunity to accomplish your goals. Saturn
doesn't really cause too many problems.

However, when Mars moves into Virgo, it can be
more challenging to deal with. Be careful of how you
act to avoid making trouble for yourself. Starting on
the 11th, Mars will test your ability to stick to a plan.
Before you start, use your past experience. Take some
time to think about what you're being given, even if it
seems boring.

Love

You're nice, but you don't move forward. You
watch what happens and how people react. This month,

the other people in your life will have to work harder than usual to win your heart. Some will go all out in their declarations of love, while others will do everything they can.

There's a lot of interest now that Mars is in Virgo. You may feel pressure from your partner to make a commitment, and your aloof demeanor could be a reason for their mistrust. Your best friend now is resistance.

Single Pisces, It's all because of your efforts! It brings you into contact with people who can entice you in different ways. This month, passion comes to you without you trying.

Career

You've been moving forward without any trouble for a few weeks. You have it easy in every way! If something goes wrong, you know what to do. From the 11th, you should be careful about how you act. Take the time to think about what to do, especially if someone from your past makes you an offer. Think about what you've done and what you've accomplished since this time. If you do this, you'll use the best attitude that won't make anyone unhappy.

Despite your efforts, it does not appear that you will achieve your objectives. There would be risks involved in some of your plans and efforts. Under these conditions, avoiding taking any kind of risk would be best.

There is also a good amount of travel shown. But again, you wouldn't get the gains you were hoping for. Even so, you might be able to get something out of a trip to the North. A month that doesn't look good for your career.

Finance

From a financial point of view, this sector works like a charm because your activities make a lot of money.

This month, businesses and companies that deal with other countries or associations between states will do very well. In fact, most of you could be working on new business deals, proposals, and financial contracts that would benefit you.

Also, the climate would be good for investing and starting new businesses. So, if you have plans like this, you should move them forward. Partnerships and professional groups also tend to cause less trouble.

Health

A great month when the stars are aligned to give you good health. You will not only stay healthy, but you will also look great because your body is getting the most out of what you eat. This is the way things should be in a good month.

Not only will you be active and full of energy throughout the month, but those who are proud of their reproductive abilities will be pleasantly surprised to find that they are, if anything, above average. This could improve your physical, emotional, and mental well-being, putting you in a good mood. The stars want you to be happy throughout this month.

Travel

A month when you won't make much money from travelling because the stars are all against you getting this blessing. Those who travel a lot for business or official work would fall into this category. At the end of the month, these people may not have much to show for their travels.

Even if things were normal, business travel wouldn't be as profitable as it would be in a typical month. Even going in the most helpful direction, which is North, wouldn't have the usual effect. Artists, writers, singers, and people like them would find their travels mostly empty and unproductive.

Insight from the stars

Do not allow anything to derail your progress; instead, maintain your current speed and rhythm. You will be ecstatic when you see the results of your hard work pay off. In everything you do, rely on your intuition. Consider the consequences of your actions before taking action.

August 2023

Horoscope

In a relaxed setting, you can progress at your own pace. Continued support from Uranus and Jupiter will help you to grow and expand while protecting your successes. Opportunities will present themselves, and you should take advantage of them because they will have no consequences. Saturn, on the other hand, provides you with the time you need to accomplish your goals.

On the other hand, Mars and Mercury in Virgo can make you more upset than you should be. Be careful of too much discouragement and running away at the wrong time. Find the right balance for this to work out well for you. Be careful not to overestimate your abilities, as they aren't limitless. Take a break if things get too tense. Also, stay away from the heated discussions that are sure to ensue.

Love

Your attitude seems a little far away, and you're not sure you want to commit. This can make people react in unexpected ways and start heated conversations. But you can stay away from them. How? By focusing on the good things in life instead of the bad, you can help each other.

Criticism comes from everywhere. A contentious subject isn't going to get your attention, sadly. By the end of the month, even the tensest situations will have calmed down considerably. As a result, you'll be in a better position to negotiate and come to an agreement with your spouse.

Single Pisces, You will probably meet people who want to help this month. Before you start, think about whether you also want a serious relationship. This will keep you from making a mistake that will make you look bad.

Career

Helpful influxes keep this sector going. You don't have to worry. On the other side, you need to be cautious about your own reactions and decisions. This month, you may be influenced by situations beyond your control to make unwise decisions. To avoid making a bad decision, you need to step aside from the opinions of others. Trust your intuition and use your experience.

If you put in the time and effort, you won't be able to attain the goals you set out to accomplish. This would have a depressing effect on you.

The stars say that traveling this month is for business or service. But again, the benefits that were hoped for might not happen. In general, having contacts would also be very useful. Although, it would be best to depend mostly on your skills and hard work. Overall, it is a month, which doesn't look good for your job prospects.

Finance

When it comes to money, it's the same fight! The only taste you should follow is your own, not the likes of others. You'll be more likely to purchase items that meet your tastes and preferences if you follow this strategy rather than the opposite.

The stars have nothing outstanding to say about your money situation this month. Almost every dispute or lawsuit you might be involved in would go against you. Try to get a decision put off until a later, better time.

People who do business with the government would have to go through a rough patch, as would those who do business with other countries or between states. In short, you would have to work hard and struggle to achieve the planned goals, and even if you did your best, you wouldn't have much success. There isn't much hope for pending loan applications or steps for new advances from banks and financial institutions.

Health

A month in which you will have to take extra care of your health to make up for the lack of blessings from the heavens. You could get sudden, severe illnesses, which would be scary. Aside from this, there may be times when your body seems to get no benefit from eating healthy food.

This wouldn't be too bad by itself and would only last for a short time. Don't worry; try to find ways to improve things, which is possible. A rough patch, for sure, but one that can be worked through with a bit of extra care and won't have any long-term effects.

Travel

During the month, you won't be able to get the usual benefits from travelling because the stars don't look good. If your job or business requires you to travel a lot, this may not amount to much this month.

Even if you didn't have to work, most travel during
this time wouldn't be enjoyable or bring you any
significant gains. In some situations, it could even
make things worse. This would be true even for trips to
the West, which is the best direction. Some of you
would lose a lot more money if you went on a business
trip overseas.

Insight from the stars

It's possible that your peace of mind could be in
jeopardy. You're free to keep it, though. How? By
coming up with a compromise that makes everyone
happy and keeps your freedom. You'll find yourself
apologizing to those you've harmed and pleading for
forgiveness. Moving on with your life without remorse
is possible if you make atonement.

September 2023

Horoscope

You've been given the opportunity to learn and grow in an environment that is ideal for your development. But you'll have to deal with Mercury and the Sun in Virgo's dissonances.

Don't try to get away when things get hard. Don't base your decisions on what other people say. Don't think that bad things just happen to you. Instead, take the time to figure out what's going on. Think about it until you know what it means. It might seem like a lot of work, but if you do it, you'll find that you're much more capable than you think.

The key to your success this month is articulating your goals and aspirations to people in a straightforward manner.

Love

Commitment gives life to your thoughts and the thoughts of others. Your friends and family may grow impatient while they wait for you. Your gentle words or gestures would be much appreciated! You might think that all of this is unimportant, but it is for the average person.

Don't leave your partner's questions unanswered. This month, grab your courage with both hands and find a way to say what you're feeling. Why? Because it will keep you from being all by yourself.

Single Pisces, You've got someone about to do something under your spell. At the same time, another person you admire is on the lookout for a tranquil getaway. Instead of avoiding these two people, consider what you actually want in life.

Career

Jupiter's presence in Taurus continues to have a positive and calming effect on this area. It's all good. However, Mercury in Virgo, which is also retrograde until the 15th, will wreak havoc on your plans. Pisces, your strategy will be thwarted by finicky brains. On the worst days, there are a lot of critics. If you think about this, especially around the 15th, you will make the wrong choice. Wait until the end of the month instead.

To succeed, you should rely solely on your abilities and efforts. This would be even more important if the course of events did not favor the achievement of your objectives.

.

Finance

If you want to buy something, don't worry about what other people like. According to the stars, this is an unlucky month for your finances. Writers, painters, sculptors, and other creative types should plan for a very slow period because that is what will happen.

Despite being friends with some intelligent, bright individuals, you will struggle to achieve your goals, and even if you do, you won't have much success. Loan applications or proposals from banks or other financial institutions are unlikely to succeed. " Plans for growth or a new enterprise should be put on hold for the time being since the current climate does not favor such endeavors."

Health

A good month, when the stars are in your favor, and your health stays good. People prone to long-term conditions like rheumatism and complaints like too much gas in the digestive tract will feel much better.

The body will use the food well, and all of the nutrients
will be taken in.

In this happy situation, you'll have a lot of chances
to live a much fuller and better life. Not only in better
shape physically but also in a much happier state of
mind and heart.

Travel

The stars are not aligned in a way that makes this a
good month for travel. Artists, actors, poets, and others
in the same line of work would find that their trips to
do their jobs don't lead anywhere.

People whose jobs or businesses require them to
travel a lot may also be disappointed because they may
not be able to do as well as they should. People who
work in sales and marketing may feel this hurts the
most. There are also signs that a trip to another country
during this time would be just as useless.

Insight from the stars

You have the option to remove yourself from
situations or people. But only if it's to take stock and
lead to a positive outcome. Pisces in business, you keep
thinking about growing your businesses. It's a fantastic

idea to grow your business, but you must be willing to
put in the effort.

October 2023

Horoscope

You've been living for a while in a safe world that keeps your knowledge and unique personality safe. But you may feel like your life is being trampled on the spot. You might feel kind of bored as it can creep up on you in various ways.

Mars in Scorpio, which starts on the 13th, allows you to push the limits of what is possible. He tells you to use your skills and do something that will help you grow personally and financially. Due to the dissonances caused by Venus in Virgo, however, you might hesitate or turn down these options.

If you don't want to do anything you'll regret, you should wait until Mercury leaves Scorpio on the 23rd. So be patient if you don't want to make a mistake. In addition to your preferences, it will allow you to make a decision based on the preferences of others.

Love

Your family or spouse isn't sure if they can trust you to stick with something. This month, it's how you make them feel that hurts them. You can only tell them what they want to hear until the 22nd. But then you say something honest that gets things back on track.

You can only keep the peace if you're willing to make some sacrifices. Unfortunately, your partner is still unconvinced about your plans for the future of your relationship. Mercury helps you put all your cards on the table at the end of the month.

Single Pisces, People who want to settle down and people who want to try new things are both drawn to you. So, you stay away and keep hoping to find the right person. This little miracle could happen this month.

Career

The job market in this area is thriving. Sadly, Virgo's dissonances disrupt this pleasant and beneficial atmosphere. Avoid listening to others' comments if you're interested in an offer that's been made to you by someone else. Reconnect with your famous intuition and trust it. Wait until the 23rd if you're not sure. In Scorpio, you'll know exactly what to do and will make your decision without regret or guilt.

It's hard to say that you'll be lucky this month because you'll have to work hard for all the good things that will happen. Relax and enjoy the positive energy. Most of the good things that will happen at work will call for a party. So, if you're interested in your career, this is something you'd love to see. If you receive job offers, promotions, or see a rise in your business income, you may be confident that you will be able to meet your financial responsibilities.

Finance

Make your own decisions when it comes to money, and do not rely on other people's recommendations. You'll make a lot of money, but you'll have to save for the bad days. You aren't in a position to splurge on frivolous or pointless purchases at the moment.

Being thrifty will be a huge asset for you. You should only buy the things you absolutely need, just like a mother would. At this time, your success will not be tied to money. You'll get favors, but they'll be based more on relationships and sentiments than anything else.

Health

The stars are shining brightly on your health this month, so take advantage. Your body and mind would profit significantly from a diet rich in vitamins and minerals, as your system would be able to utilize these nutrients to their maximum potential. In fact, even the finest of your, mental, physical, and creative powers would remain intact.

However, there are some reasons why you shouldn't push yourself too hard. A reasonable schedule that doesn't put too much stress on you would be more than enough. A positive outlook and feeling upbeat would keep you physically active and energized throughout the month.

Travel

During this month, the wisest among you can drastically cut back on your travel plans to avoid the harmful effects of the stars, which will keep you from making big money through travel. People who have to travel a lot for work or business may be the ones who suffer the most.

But it's comforting to know that these things will lead to better times. Artists, singers, dancers, and others like them may not get the usual benefits from their travels, either. Exporters and others who work with countries outside of the U.S. should also try to avoid going abroad as much as possible since they might not get much out of it.

Insight from the stars

Making compromises may alleviate some of your frustration, but it does little to motivate you. If you want to progress, seize the moment while it is still in front of you. You'll finally be able to appreciate all of your hard work. You've waited long enough, and now amazing things are about to come your way.

November 2023

Horoscope

This month, the Scorpion energies will keep pushing you to go even further. With the help of planets in the signs of Taurus and Capricorn, you can pull off this small miracle. Unfortunately, the dissonances caused by the planets' moving through Sagittarius will put up barriers you will have to overcome.

If you agree, your condition may improve this month. To do this, you should not consider the problems you will face as fatalities but as challenges. Don't worry if you have doubts. There is nothing you can't overcome. Take your time and avoid getting caught up in the task at hand. Follow your gut and take things one step at a time.

Love

Commitment is a cause for worry until the 8th. Then you try to find good middle ground. Unfortunately, you probably have some problems.

Instead of getting lost by making plans for a perfect world, be direct. Think about yourself instead of always thinking about other people.

It's not easy to be in your relationship. Thanks to compromises, things are getting better between you both. Even if you find an answer that works for everyone, ensure it doesn't hurt you.

Single Pisces, It's easy to woo people who want to settle down. On the other hand, it takes persistence to catch that special someone. You can choose between a perfect life and a lasting relationship this month. If you stay calm, what you want will come true.

Career

This month, you can change the path of your career. You might get a different job or work in a country outside of your country. If your career is changing, Pisces, there's a good reason. So stop putting yourself down or thinking you won't be able to do the job. If you need to, contact someone who will teach you everything. They will try to get you to take this opportunity when it comes up.

This shows that you're in charge of your career and are going at your speed. You want to make your dreams come true, and you want to make sure you do. You're ready for a challenge, and there will be a lot of good opportunities for you. Your drive and ambition will take you places, and you'll have great memories from your business trips.

Finance

On the money side, if you need to make a big purchase, ask other people what they think and then choose based on what you like. This could mean stability in terms of money and work. This month will be clear and give you confidence. It will help your finances because your gut will tell you where to put your money in business.

Don't get into fights about money, as this can greatly affect your financial situation.

Health

A month in which you would have to pay a lot of attention to your health to make up for the absence of any heavenly blessings during this month. During this month, you might see signs of wasting, which is when the body isn't able to use much of what it eats, even if it's healthy food. There's no need to worry because this could be fixed with the right medicine.

Your ability to reproduce may also be down, but again, this is just a bad effect of the stars that will only

last for a while. This could be quickly remedied when
you are much stronger.

A time during which you should be careful and take
the proper steps to keep yourself from worrying and
keep your mind at ease throughout this time

Travel

According to the stars, this month is not a good time
to travel. Not only would it not be profitable, but it
could even cost you extra money. On your trips, you
could get hurt or have some other kind of physical
trouble. This is especially true for those who like to
take risks and try new things.

Even if nothing else went wrong, the trips taken this
month would not produce the expected results. Even
trips in the best direction toward the West would be the
same. The same thing will happen on trips abroad.
Because these trips are expensive, they can sometimes
make your losses much worse.

Insight from the stars

You can expand your sphere of influence. Do not
allow yourself to be swayed by ease if you want to
achieve this little miracle. Opt to excel and surpass

yourself instead. Weak immunity necessitates extreme
caution when it comes to your health.

December 2023

Horoscope

The energies of Taurus and Capricorn always help you rise to the top. Venus, who will be in Scorpio from the 5th to the 29th, has replaced Mars in Scorpio as the planet of support. Despite your lack of willpower, your intuition has been bolstered. Your emotions will serve as your best guide. Your life takes a turn for the better, thanks to the support of your family and friends.

Mars will add to the problems that come from Sagittarius until December 31. If you really want to get what you want, you will have to fight against these energies. To do well at this little trick, be nice to people who have been with you for a long time and distance yourself from people who bring you down.

Love

The energies of Sagittarius can make you lose control of yourself. Venus in Scorpio steps in to help you get back on the right track. Even though it will be hard, try to ignore outside influences this month. Give people with their heads on their shoulders more of your time.

There are still issues in your relationship that could get you in trouble. To avoid this, you must have the wisdom to divide your life into sections. Put yourself and your partner in a safe space. You won't have to be concerned about anything after that.

Single Pisces, Because you live in different worlds, you meet different people. Think about what you really want before making a decision. This will keep you from getting involved in a relationship that could hurt you.

Career

Jupiter still favors this sector. As it retrogrades, you'll have more time to organize your affairs so that you don't have to worry about it more than necessary. However, relying on the advice of others should be avoided because it can lead to poor decisions. Fighting isn't in your blood, Pisces, but you'll do it if the situation calls for it. So, don't be afraid to say no to things that aren't right for you.

An uninspiring month for your professional advancement. Work may be enjoyable, but it is doubtful that promised rewards would materialize after many hours of diligent effort.

This month, contacts won't be very useful. Because of this, it would be best to rely mostly on your skills to get out of challenging situations. You wouldn't get what you expected from travel, but a trip to the North would be good for you. Overall, this is a month in which you must be cautious and rely on your efforts.

Finance

On the money side, if you want to make someone happy, you should do it before December 27th, because the Full Moon will make it hard for you to understand how you feel.

A good month for your finances, during which you could make a lot of money, but not without any problems. The success of your projects, no matter what they are, would be boosted by your friendships with smart, spiritually-minded people. In fact, this would give your whole work life a satisfying level of culture and refinement.

You'd be able to achieve most of your goals and make the most money from them. Still, you'll likely run into problems along the way. But success is sure to happen. A good time to not only get a lot done but also to feel a lot of satisfaction.

Health

A month in which your health is good, and you really don't have much to worry about. Your body would get the most out of what you eat, so not only would it be healthy, but it would also look healthy. This would make you very busy and full of energy.

In fact, those of you who like to test your fitness ability would be pleasantly surprised to find that, if anything, your physical skills are way above average during this time. This would make for a pretty full life, with more and better things to enjoy. The only thing that stands out, and there is one, is the chance of an accident or a severe injury, which should be taken care of. But this is a long shot.

Travel

Since the stars are in your favor, this is a month when you can expect to make a lot of money from your travels. There are signs that the way things are going will force you to travel a lot for work. If you did these things, you would be successful. The North would be the best direction to go.

These are more signs that any trip you take abroad in the month will also help you reach your goals. Those who have been thinking about taking such a trip should go now.

Insight from the stars

Your success will depend on how well you stay on the right path. This month, pay attention to people who share your values. Everything will be fine if you do this. Don't settle for less than what you can do because you can do great things. Always try to do your best. Even during the Mercury retrograde in 2023, you will do great things that will surprise you.